Y0-BVR-609

WINNING
ON THE
TELEPHONE

Donald H. Weiss

amacom
American Management Association

This book is available at a special
discount when ordered in bulk quantities.
For information, contact Special Sales Department,
AMACOM, a division of
American Management Association,
135 West 50th Street, New York, NY 10020.

Library of Congress Cataloging-in-Publication Data

Weiss, Donald H., 1936–
     Winning on the telephone.
     (The Successful office skills series)
     Includes index.
     1. Telephone in business.   I. Title.   II. Series.
HF5541.T4W44   1988   651.7'3   88-47700
ISBN 0-8144-7699-6

© 1988 AMACOM, a division of
American Management Association, New York.
All rights reserved.
Printed in the United States of America.

This publication may not be reproduced,
stored in a retrieval system,
or transmitted in whole or in part,
in any form or by any means, electronic,
mechanical, photocopying, recording, or otherwise,
without the prior written permission of AMACOM,
a division of American Management Association,
135 West 50th Street, New York, NY 10020.

Printing number

10 9 8 7 6 5 4 3

CONTENTS

Introduction

How Important Is the Telephone in Your Job?

A phone begins to ring the second Les Hobart walks into the marketing department's space. A quick glance confirms that he stands alone in the room. Although the calls have been forwarded to the receptionist, he picks up the receiver on the second ring anyway:

Les: Hello?

Voice: This is Alice Beeman. Is Marti Powers available?

Les: No. No one's here.

Voice: Have you any idea of when she'll be back?

Les: No.

Voice: [*Irritated*] Would you take a message, please? It's important.

Les: [*Scanning the desktop*] Haven't got a message pad handy.

Voice: [*Sounding a lot more irritated*] Would you tell Marti I called, please? Ask her to call me back. It's about our order.

Les: Yeah. Sure.

After hanging up, Les searches the desk at which he is standing. Not finding a message pad there, he departs without leaving a note for Marti.

Within a minute of digging into his stack of work in the graphics department, Les forgets all about the call. Just as well, in one regard: He hasn't remembered the caller's name, anyway.

The story doesn't end there, naturally. You know Marti took some heat from Alice Beeman when the direct marketing supervisor didn't return the call. Marti also took it from her manager when she found out about it.

Yes, the caller complained. Have you ever been in Alice Beeman's shoes? Not only was Les rude and monosyllabic, he also ignored her statement that the call was important. Yet, he left no message.

Has anything like that ever happened where you work? Probably not exactly; but something similar to poor phone handling and a missed message has happened to almost everyone.

The most vital role in the communication network that the business telephone has become makes poor phone handling and missed messages a serious problem. Written communication has taken a backseat, especially with the advent of features such as conference calling, speed dialing, remote-control answering machines, and teleconferencing.

To find out just how vital the phone is to you or your work unit, ask yourself these questions: How many times a day do you or your employees talk business on the phone? Once? Twice? Dozens? Why? Who does the calling and what do you talk about? What features does your phone system have that increase its utility? What would happen if you disconnected the telephone?

Assuming that you've pronounced the phone vital, take a look at the results you usually get. How often do you hang up and say, "I wish I had said . . ." or "Why'd I agree to that?" or "Wow! He talked my ear off!" or, "I couldn't get a thing out of her"?

As important to communicating as is this marvel of engineering, it often seems surprising to hear how poorly people use the telephone. You've heard the mumblers or shouters at the other end of the line, too.

How about people who talk so fast that you have no idea what they are saying? Or who talk so slowly you lose their train of thought before they finish their sentence? How about the monotones who put you to sleep while announcing that you've just won the lottery?

Then, again, why be surprised? Most organizations don't give much thought to how people come across; or, if they do think about it, such thoughts are usually reduced to a memo: "Be prompt, courteous, helpful, . . ." But they don't train their employees in what they expect or want or in how to use the telephone.

Well, after you read this little book, you'll be able to make more effective calls, take control of calls that interfere with what you're doing, handle some of the more obnoxious calls you get, and speak and listen more effectively over the phone. If you already win on the telephone, you can use this book to help others do the same.

I'll help you achieve those objectives by talking about them, and, through the story, will illustrate both the mistakes people make and the things they do (or should do) right. Les, a graphic arts supervisor, works with Marti and Albert for Wilson Packaging Company, a fictitious organization. Les, Marti, and Albert are fictitious, too, but they're drawn from numerous real-life cases.

What they do and say, real people do and say. The events described at the beginning of this Introduction happened. Once the real Marti found out who had angered her client, it didn't happen a second time.

Chapter 1

Why the Telephone Works Against You

You can't live without it anymore, but oh, can the telephone get you into trouble! Like any other electronic gadget, of course, it's just there, an inanimate object, an instrument to be used. Usually, however, it's not the machine that creates the problem. As the computer people say, "Garbage in, garbage out."

But, our ear's extension comes with built-in liabilities

and obstacles to overcome. We use the telephone to complete a communication in an incomplete communication environment.

Everyone either makes calls or takes them. Either way, listening and speaking go on in an often noisy environment in which the people trying to communicate lose both the advantage of visual cues and control over a part of the physical setting. Noise, together with loss of cues and loss of control, increases the chances for hard-to-undo mistakes and misunderstandings. When we lose the advantage of visual cues, we lose factual data and information about feelings and emotions.

Loss of Visual Cues

Consider the obvious. Here's Les on the phone again, impatiently talking with another client who doesn't have the time to wait for a picture to be sent in the mail—not even by overnight express. "Listen, the logo's a monogram," Les says. "Royal blue. You'll like it, believe me."

Why should the client believe him? He or she can't see Les's environment and can't see what he's referring to. Any communication that includes references to physical things suffers from this absence of vision.

So much for the obvious. The lack of vision also causes problems for salespeople and others who have to make judgments about people and their needs.

Albert, one of Wilson's top salespeople, is calling prospects to follow up on a mass mailing:

Albert: As you saw in the flier, the filing system's built out of corrugated cardboard. Four small boxes with replaceable labels that slide easily in and out of their compartments. Lightweight and easy to use, it sits right on top of the desk where you have ready access to it.

Prospect: Don't know that it would do me much good. Don't know where I'd put it, what with a computer, a printer, stack trays, a

---

Environmental Losses

- Visual cues
- Silent gestures
- Context
- Control

---

telephone, and a calculator on my desk already.

It's difficult to relate to and communicate with someone without seeing the kind of world that surrounds that person—not just the cluttered desktop, but also how he or she decorates that world—because decor signals values and interests.

When deciding on what personal benefit to explain to a prospect, knowing what the other person believes is important helps you decide what to talk about. The life of a telephone salesperson is no picnic, but telephone salespeople are not alone in needing this type of information.

We often have to persuade someone to make a decision or do something. Showing that person how the decision or action will benefit him or her usually helps us get what we want or need, e.g., support for a proposal or a policy change. What we see in the person's surroundings tips us off to what he or she would value or find a benefit. Clearly, our opportunities for picking up on the right cues are limited by the lack of visual information.

Silent Gestures or Nonverbals

Visual contexts and impressions are only part of what we lose when we talk on the telephone. Silent gestures (nonverbals) help communicate meanings.

Everyone grows up using facial expressions and hand movements to communicate important messages. We stand in certain ways, sit in certain ways.

All of our gestures are culturally defined or are defined by more immediate groups, e.g., families or ethnic groups, and, in essence, they're automatic.

Les is still talking with the client about the logo. "The S is scrolled." As he speaks, he waves his finger in the air to approximate a scrolled S. "You don't know what that looks like, huh? Hmm. I don't know how else to describe it. You don't happen to have a facsimile receiver, do you?"

What earthly good did it do Les or the client for our graphic arts supervisor to wave his finger in the air to someone who can't see it? Broad gestures make for obvious examples, but we do the same things with subtle shades of meaning that our silent gestures provide.

To understand for yourself how important silent gestures are, take some time to observe people talking on the phone. Watch how they emphasize words by hand gestures or make faces, shake, or nod their heads as if the person on the other end can see them. It's simply too hard to talk without silent gestures.

Meaningful Sounds

Since neither party to a telephone call sees visual cues, he or she must rely on other cues to collect all the meanings associated with the spoken words. Mostly, the other cues are meaningful sounds (quasi-verbals).

Tone of voice, pitch, and volume qualify as meaningful sounds. Each person infers from those expressions what the other person feels about what he or she is saying, or about you, or about the situation. Loud, high-pitched, harsh tones signify anger to most people. Loud, high-pitched laughter signifies joy, although some nervous, frightened people sound this way. But it is the sound coupled with the context that helps us interpret the sound's meaning, so the loss of context on the telephone makes interpretation difficult.

Still, speech mannerisms help us speculate about the other person, just as he or she is speculating about us. We've learned to interpret sounds to mean certain

6

things. For example, someone we know may ordinarily speak without difficulty; yet, during a conference call, the person may stammer. We conclude from what we hear that the person is feeling pressured.

You've noticed that people throw in a lot of extra "ers" and "ahs" when talking on the phone, haven't you? Maybe you throw them in, too. One interpretation suggests that they're trying to think of what to say. Another interpretation states that they're using the sounds to control the flow of the exchange, filling the silence that would otherwise allow you to talk. At least, that's how some people interpret things.

Regardless of how we interpret a situation, we base what we think or feel on what we hear and how the other person sounds to us.

Some sounds can encourage us to talk—e.g., "hum," "uh huh." Or they can discourage us—e.g., "mm mm," "ugh," "bah." We've been taught that the sounds (and often the tone in which they're made) tell us to go on or stop talking. At the same time, those sounds can signify completely different meanings—for example, "hmm" could be a cover for disinterest.

Danger lurks in any interpretation based on mere sounds. We have to interpret silent gestures, also, that's true, and because silent gestures are ambiguous and unclear, we should check out what someone means by them. So, lose the ability to see what's happening, and the ambiguities and muddiness increase.

As I discuss in detail later, all interpretations contain assumptions, values, or memories of previous experience that may have little or nothing to do with the other person's intent. When we're left with nothing but words and quasi-verbal sounds to interpret, instead of communicating with someone, we're often locked up in our own minds guessing at what he or she means. Poor business, the telephone.

Losing Control of the Physical Environment

The telephone is especially poor business because who knows or controls what's really going on at the other end of the line? What we don't know and can't control can hurt us.

When we get on the phone to talk with someone, we not only often misinterpret or misunderstand, we also automatically lose control over a part of the physical environment in which we're trying to communicate.

When you sit down together in another person's office, you can get him or her to close the door, forward the telephone, and ignore the noise in the hall. Try controlling the physical environment *at the other end of the line during a phone conversation.* Fat chance!

That's the other person's world, and during the conversation, he or she can let his or her environment interfere. Someone comes into the room, and he or she pays attention to the interloper, not to you. You can't know what's happening until it becomes clear that you've lost contact.

A common loss of control occurs when the other person lets his or her mind wander. Some people doodle absentmindedly and, without realizing it, become absorbed in the doodle; but you can't know that, either. Not until they neglect to answer your question or respond to a comment does it become clear.

Let's look in on a conversation between Marti and Alice Beeman. Marti took care of the earlier problem, but now she's having problems of her own:

Marti: We shipped four hundred of those containers last week. They should arrive today.

Alice: Oh, wait a minute, Marty. Don't bring those in here.

Marti: [*Confusion registering on her face as well as in her voice*] What's that?

Alice: Take them to the supply room.

Marti: What are you talking about?

Alice: We really need those boxes, Marti.

Marti: Yes, I understand that. We shipped—

Alice: Thanks, Marty.

Marti: What?

Alice: I'm sorry, Marti. Everything happens at once. You know how it is. But as I was saying, we need those boxes. We can't get our orders out

Marti: without them, and we're falling behind. Hold on a second, Marti. Help Marty get those things out of here.

Marti: Alice, you have me so confused, I have no idea what we're talking about.

When Marti is frustrated or anxious, she doodles to relieve her tension. Very frustrated by Alice's ramblings, she begins to doodle furiously on her desk pad. The doodle takes the shape of a woman's profile—a woman with a long, pointed nose. "It looks just like Alice," Marti chuckles to herself.

Alice: Get Jerry to help. Jack, too. Marty brought 'em in. Marti, please. Help us like you used to. If we don't get those boxes, we're in deep trouble. [*When Marti doesn't answer immediately, but chuckles instead, Alice repeats herself*] Do you hear me, Marti? We need those boxes.

Marti: Oh, yes, Alice. I understand that. We shipped—

Alice: I can't hear you, Marti. They brought all those things in here instead of taking them to the supply room. Now they're throwing them around, angry at me because I want them out of here. I can't understand those supply-room people.

Can you see to it that our order's shipped, Marti? I could always count on you before you were promoted. I wish they'd find us a replacement to handle our account. Now that you're supervising direct marketing, we don't get any of the service we've come to expect from your firm.

With most of what Alice said swallowed by the background noise in her office, Marti is at a loss for what to say.

Marti: What was that, Alice? I can't hear you.

Alice: Oh, never mind, Marti. Just get that order shipped.

Marti: It was. Last week.

Alice:	What?
Marti:	It was shipped last week.
Alice:	You say you'll get it shipped?
Marti:	It was shipped last week.
Alice:	We should expect it next week?
Marti:	Today.
Alice:	[*Snapping*] Well! Good day to you, too.

When Marti hears the other receiver bang, she knows she has another problem with Alice Beeman to solve.

Poor Marti. Most things that could go wrong with a phone conversation did—distractions, noise, loss of attention, and loss of control. A great many things can happen in the other person's world over which you have no control.

Then there are our own interpretations of what we think is happening in the other world. The other party is distracted; we take that as disinterest and become upset. He or she may be in the middle of something important and need to get on with it; we take his or her tone of voice for hostility, although it may really mean only mild impatience. We react not to what's happening but rather to what we *think* is happening, and the problem escalates.

That din in Alice's background drowned out what was said, but at least she and Marti kept asking each other for clarification (not that it did either of them any good). What if for some reason the other person doesn't ask you to repeat yourself? Or worse, the noise drowns out what he or she says and you fail to ask the person to repeat it?

That's what happened when Albert took an order last week from a long-time customer. "What do you mean you didn't order six thousand boxes? You most certainly did. When you called last Thursday from the plant. I could hardly hear you over that din." He listened, ashen-faced. "You said six *hundred*? You need six *hundred,* not six thousand? Well, I could've sworn you said six thousand."

So no one ever calls you from the floor of a factory. Did you ever try talking through crossed wires or static or echoes? The telephone medium itself produces wonderful noise. And, static and crossed wires aside, the wire distorts the voice. Overtones and subtleties are lost.

Lose control over any necessary part of a complex process, and you buy trouble. Since effective communication is a complex process, you can bet the telephone's incomplete communication environment increases the chances for mistakes and misunderstandings that are harder to undo than are face-to-face communication problems.

You'd think that because no social contact exists without some kind of communication, controlling it would be relatively easy, but that isn't so. Its complexity makes bridling it that much more difficult.

Take the case of not saying anything. What could be simpler than not talking at all? But not talking sends messages, whether you consciously send them or not, and silence often conveys something you don't intend. When you're on the telephone, your silence—even a deliberate pause to give the other person an opportunity to say something—is easily misinterpreted to mean you're distracted.

What you don't see can hurt you, and distractions or distortions affect how the other person interprets what you say or don't say.

Chapter 2

How the Telephone Changes the Communication Process

I've been talking about Murphy's Law of the telephone: Whatever can go wrong will go wrong at some time or another. So, how do you cut your losses? Since telephoning's nothing more than an attempt to communicate, what is there about that complex process itself

Trying to communicate completely in an incomplete environment.

that you can use to gain more control over that environment? The answer: Control the structure of your messages and the filters that interfere with reaching a consensus of meaning.

The process as a whole consists of two people trying to communicate with each other. In a two-way telephone conversation, both parties alternate roles of message sender with message receiver. They encode and decode messages; they filter meanings in and they filter them out; they struggle through various barriers and obstacles; and lo and behold, they come to the end of their conversation fairly confident that they've understood each other.

Sending and Receiving Messages

Take a look at Figure 1. It represents a model of unconstrained, face-to-face communication, the ideal of communication—which, needless to say, telephone talking isn't.

The crossing lines connecting the figures' eyes, ears, and faces represent the fact that both people send messages—words, meaningful sounds, and silent gestures—the other receives. When someone sends a message, that person *en*codes his or her ideas, beliefs, feelings, emotions, values, or attitudes, putting them into words or some other mode of expression that is meaningful *to that person*.

When the other party receives the message, he or she *de*codes or *interprets* the message by turning the sounds or gestures that represent the first person's ideas, beliefs, feelings, emotions, values, or attitudes into words or some other mode of expression that is *meaningful to him or her*.

Figure 1. The communication process.

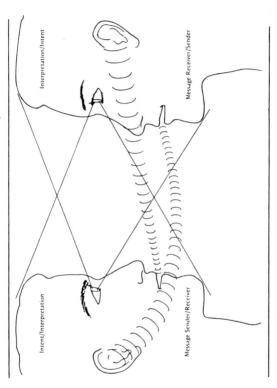

Interpretation/Intent

Message Receiver/Sender

Intent/Interpretation

Message Sender/Receiver

The structure of the message introduces the first complication into the process. Every message consists of content and expression—what the message is trying to convey and how it conveys it.

Usually we use words to transmit information (content). "This is a book." "I feel happy." "You're standing on my foot." In business, when we talk on the phone, our primary objective consists of communicating content. Yet, we frequently let our tone of voice, inflection, pacing, and emphasis transmit expressive intent and obscure the content of the message.

Expressive intent accompanies every verbal message (content), regardless of what that message is. And, this is one area in which we can control the telephone process, because most of the time we are able to separate expression from content as we talk.

Sometimes you want expressive intent to dominate the message, as when you're expressing an important emotion or feeling. Letting someone know you're angry or pleased requires that you tell them not only with the words you use but also by the way you express those words. "I think your product's the best on the market," spoken with all the inflections of a robot doesn't seem very sincere. "I insist you get our order shipped immediately," spoken in a hushed (rather than hissed) whisper doesn't have much impact.

Although people can separate the two modes of communication, they don't always try. Sometimes, without realizing it, they communicate expressive intent through meaningful sounds (quasi-verbals). They think they're sending a message with content, but their tone of voice or speech mannerisms are sending a different or additional message that clouds or hides the content. Either their use of quasi-verbals or the receiver's interpretation of them has gotten in the way of the content they're trying to get across, and the content is not received as intended. Then, they have serious problems.

Only by paying attention to *how* we express ourselves (as opposed to *what* we say) can we separate expressiveness from content. We need to hear our tone of voice, pitch, tempo, and volume through other people's ears.

Two ways of doing that are having a trusted person tell you how you sound, and whether or not your expression covers your content, and listening to yourself on a tape recorder. I'll talk about this later, also.

Now, let's take a look at what just one quasi-verbal can do to a message. Marti is on the phone with the mailroom supervisor. In the course of the conversation, she says, "I need that mailing list right now." How many different ways do you think *emphasis* affects the words' meaning?

Take a pencil and paper and rewrite that sentence with as many different emphases as you can. Underline the word or phrase you're emphasizing. For example, "*I* need that mailing list right now." What does that emphasis convey to you?

When you've finished making your list of emphases and their meanings, take a look at some of the possibilities we identify in Exhibit 1. When you finish reading our interpretations, continue reading here.

Interesting? Well, something else compounds the problem. It's not always your expressive *intent* that's communicated; sometimes your emphasis distorts your intent. Sometimes *how the other person interprets the emphasis* distorts its meaning. As a result of their lack of clarity and their ambiguity, quasi-verbals produce mixed messages, messages that come across one way when you intend another. Over the telephone, with no visual cues to help you interpret what the other person's trying to say, meaningful sounds can hinder more often than help.

That's because quasi-verbals frequently carry with them the filters through which people send or receive messages.

Filters

Now look at the diagram shown in Figure 2. As if the telephone doesn't create enough obstacles and barriers, see how filters affect the ideal communication

Exhibit 1. The effects of emphasis.

Emphasis	Possible Meanings
"*I* need that mailing list right now."	"Don't pass it to anyone else before I get it."
"I *need* that mailing list right now."	Beseeching, pleading, or, depending on tone of voice, demanding.
"I need *that* mailing list right now."	Specifying, making clear.
"I need *that mailing list* right now."	Specifying, making clear, or, depending on tone of voice, demanding.
"I need that mailing list *right now.*"	Urgency.
"I need *that* mailing list *right now.*"	Specifying, making clear; urgency. Possibly demanding.
"I need that mailing list right now."	Demanding; possibly anger.

model. Those are the really serious obstacles and barriers between people trying to communicate. When you've taken a good look at the figure, continue reading.

Our origins and experiences birth and nurture those thick barriers, which are made up of prejudices, beliefs, feelings, emotions, values, and attitudes. Since all our encoders (words, sounds, and gestures) pass through those filters, our history invests our expression with meanings we may not know we're giving them.

What happens when other people decode our messages? That's right. The messages pass through their filters. As interpreters, they call upon their personal history to *filter in* meanings of their own and also to *filter out* the meanings we intended.

The end product isn't what we said or otherwise sent but what they *think* we sent. It's their own interpretation, regardless of what *we think* we sent.

The filters form barriers that complicate the already ambiguous environment of phone talk. Inasmuch as filters affect both encoding and decoding, it takes a

Figure 2. The communication process: Part II.

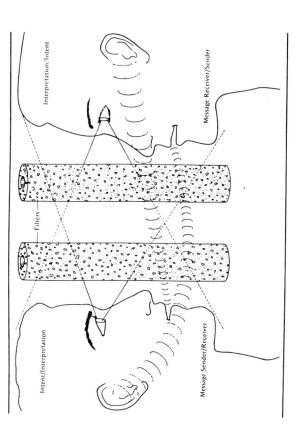

Interpretation/Intent

Message Receiver/Sender

Filters

Intent/Interpretation

Message Sender/Receiver

real effort to separate content and expressive intent. You know what it's like when you get into it with someone the way Marti and Alice are into it in this conversation:

Marti: Alice, I never told you I didn't want to talk to you.

Alice: [*Almost childishly petulant*] Yes, you did. When I called this morning you told me that.

Marti: [*Puzzled*] How did you get that out of what I said? All I said was, "I can't talk to you. I'll call you back."

Alice: [*Even more petulant*] Now that you're a supervisor, you can't talk with me. You haven't the time for me or our account. You don't want to talk with me.

Marti: [*Defensively*] I don't know what to tell you, Alice. But I meant only that I couldn't talk with you then. I was tied up with the mailroom supervisor.

Alice: Oh, well. I've got you now, so let's get on with it.

Marti and Alice may "get on with it," but they haven't resolved the issue of what Marti said. Alice filtered in her feelings about how Marti's new position seemed to her to interfere with their relationship.

Marti made matters worse with an incomplete communication in an incomplete environment—by distractedly saying *only:* "I can't talk with you. I'll call you later." Given their earlier phone conversation, Marti already felt impatient with Alice. You can imagine what that new distraction from her work did to her tone of voice. However she said "I can't talk to you," her expressiveness, intended or not, merely reinforced Alice's preconceived ideas of Marti's relationship to her.

Alice's filters jammed the phone line with bad feelings, and since she couldn't see the distraction (the mailing list with which Marti and the mailroom supervisor had been hassling), Alice simply let her own expressiveness cloud the content of Marti's message. That's how filters work.

If Alice's bad feelings linger, they may injure their vendor-customer relationship. To solve this problem, Marti must make the other woman understand what she intends—to get Alice to agree on the meaning of the message. Once they achieve a *consensus of meaning,* Alice will see the difference between what Marti meant—"I can't talk with you [*now*]"—and what she heard—"I don't *want* to talk with you."

Consensus of Meaning

Effective communication doesn't just happen, it happens only when both the sender and the receiver agree on the interpretation of a message and achieve a consensus of meaning. Sometimes that requires a great deal of effort. Two people don't have to agree that the message is true or valid, but, unless one person understands what the other means (intends), there is no communication.

Fortunately, most of the time, our natural language helps us reach consensus without ever knowing we've done it. Sharing a common language and learning common interpretations of meaningful sounds or silent gestures includes automatic consensus. Agreed-upon meanings are built into definitions, interpretations, and usage. That apparently spontaneous meeting of the minds makes communicating deceptively simple and natural. But, just like everything else about talking on the telephone, it's not as simple and as natural as it seems.

Filters get in the way of consensus, and the extent to which filters get in the way, especially unintentionally, determines how effectively we communicate. To make matters worse, filters don't come in matched pairs. No two people share exactly the same filters. As a result, we often work at, or should work at, reaching consensus.

Do you have any brothers or sisters? Then, you know how very differently people even in the same family can see the same things. You only children know how differently you and your parents see things. In fact, it seems we shouldn't talk about the "same family" or the "same things," because no two people live in the same family or experience the same anything.

Position in time and space influences our filters. Where we are and the time period in which we live cloud our filters with values, ways of seeing things, and ways of interpreting our experiences. Likewise, position in a family—whether we are an only child or are the younger sibling—also influences or affects the filters we build.

Now, if two people from the same family come away with very different sets of filters, what is it like for people from very different family cultures or other environments? Filters cause the English language to be different for two people growing up in different parts of the United States. Certain words may bear slightly different meanings for them. Gestures in one part of the country or in one family culture take on different meanings in another. What each person intends and what each person interprets may not be the same, as this little anecdote based on a real conversation suggests.

Albert, from Chicago, has just finished describing the company's new line of laser-printed labels to a customer from Southeast Texas. They've known each other a long time, and often tease back and forth:

Albert: So, Billy, how does that sound to you?
Billy: [*Drawling*] Can't rightly say. Didn't catch much of it. Sounded like y'all's fixin' to catch a train.
Albert: Now what's all that supposed to mean— "can't rightly say," "y'all," "fixin' "? What kind of language is that?
Billy: You Yankees talk too fast.
Albert: That's not it, Billy. You cowpokes hear too slow.

Two Americans, speaking the *same* language. Does reaching consensus seem as simple and natural as it did? Next chance you get, talk about speaking English with someone for whom English is a second language or with someone from another English-speaking country. Seeing how meanings, shaped by personal histories, vary should be very instructive for understanding how disagreements arise from semantic differences.

As difficult as filters make communication, it's nothing to worry about. You can, with just a little effort, gain control over your own filters and make reaching consensus a little easier. Later, I'll talk about how to help the other person control his or her filters.

Controlling Your Own Filters

You control your own filters by checking out what they contain and by checking out your own level of literacy and articulateness as well as the other person's ability to handle the language you use. But check for speech mannerisms first. They often complicate the problems filters produce.

One way to find out how you sound to someone else is to have someone you trust, someone who cares about you, talk to you about your vocal mannerisms when you speak on the telephone. Accept the feedback with an open mind. Don't defend yourself. Don't make excuses. Don't even explain why you say or do what you say or do on the phone. Just listen. You may not like what you hear, but good medicine doesn't always taste good.

Do you fall back on "ers" and "ums" to give yourself time to think? Do you use too many meaningful sounds—"Uh huh," "Hmm"—while the other person's talking? Do you speak too rapidly, or too slowly? In a monotone? Do you shout? Or do you speak too softly? Do you enunciate clearly, or do you swallow your words? All of these mannerisms, which came with you as you grew up, get in the way of effective telephone communication.

In Chapter 5, I'll have more to say about speaking mannerisms, but I suggest you begin now to practice speaking mannerisms that get the results you want. Speak at an easy-going pace with a well-modulated voice, good inflections, changes of pitch, and clear pronunciation; these mannerisms help focus a person's attention on *what,* not *how,* you're communicating.

Practice on a tape recorder. Talk, don't read. Ad lib on any subject, especially a subject related to your ordinary business conversations. Play it back. Play it for your friendly feedback partner. What can you do to make what you say sound better and more effective? Tune in to both *what* you say and *how* you say it.

Then check your filters in depth. Look at your own values, beliefs, biases, and previous experiences. The more comfortable you are with what you say—that is, what you say seems right all or most of the time—the more likely it is that what's coming out is highly filtered. The more comfortable you are with what you hear, the more likely it is that you're filtering out things you don't like or don't want to hear. What you're saying or hearing doesn't *always* have to challenge your assumptions and values, but *some* of it *should.*

What triggers emotions or feelings? When you're talking about something important, does intensity creep into your tone of voice, making you seem belligerent, angry, or demanding? Do you say things with such apparent self-assurance that you appear convinced you're right and will accept no contradiction?

Do you laugh a lot, nervously sometimes, making it sound as if you aren't taking the conversation seriously? Do you argue rather than disagree when confronted with a difference of opinion? Your friendly feedback partner can help make you aware of the emotional overtones or feeling tones that your filters contribute to your mishandling of telephone conversations.

Finally, check your own level of literacy and articulateness. You can't win on the phone if you don't understand what other people are saying. Sometimes you don't understand them because your vocabulary doesn't include words other people use all the time. In another book in this series, *How to Increase Your Reading Power,* I show you ways to build up your own storehouse of words.

Building your vocabulary will improve your ability to express yourself. If you find it difficult to choose the right words to get across what you intend, other people find it difficult to understand you. Studying how to use the right words in the right places helps you break down your filters by replacing personal definitions or turns of phrase with common or shared meanings. Reaching automatic consensus helps you overcome the built-in biases your natural language contains.

Winning on the phone requires that you use words effectively, but you must use a well-developed vocabulary carefully. The other person's level of articulateness should determine the level at which you speak. You must either speak to your audience or risk losing it; so test the other person's ability to handle the language you use.

Especially avoid jargon or technical language until you find out if your listener also speaks it. What seems perfectly simple and natural to you may sound foreign to someone else.

How to Cut Through the Filters

Let Marti illustrate how to cut through filters and get closer to reality. Even though Marti and Alice have gotten on with their business, Marti knows that the bad feelings linger on. So before their conversation ends, she raises the issue with her customer:

Marti: Listen, Alice. About your earlier call. I thought you were pretty upset about what happened.
Alice: I still am.
Marti: I understand, and I'd like us to talk about it. Okay?
Alice: I guess so. No harm can come from talking.
Marti: What made you think I didn't want to talk with you?
Alice: You didn't return my call this morning. And when I finally got through to you, you cut me off abruptly.
Marti: [*Quickly interjecting*] I see.
Alice: You *were* short with me, you know, and I didn't like the tone of voice you used.

Marti: [*Not interrupting, but indicating she's listening*] Hmm.

Alice: We've worked together for three years, Marti, and you have never been abrupt before. To tell the truth, I felt as if I was being told to get lost, that I was pestering you.

Marti: [*Hesitating for a few seconds, not sure if Alice has finished*] So, you're saying that when I didn't get right back to you, my abruptness suggested I didn't want to talk with you. My manner seemed curt or annoyed that you called, and that upset you. Is that right?

Alice: That's how it seems to me.

Marti: What else made you think I didn't want to talk with you?

Alice: [*Testy*] It only makes sense to assume that your boss wants you to ease out of our relationship. You've too much to do as a supervisor now to be bothered with old accounts.

Marti: [*Showing she is listening*] I see.

Alice: We understand that happens. After all, you have new duties now, and helping us takes you away from the new duties. So—

Marti waits, but when Alice doesn't go on, she takes this as a cue for her to say something.

Marti: Are you saying you read that assumption into my actions and tone of voice?

Alice: I guess I did. I'm sorry I did that.

Marti: I'm the one who should be truly sorry, Alice. I should have been more patient with your call. Sometimes when I get rushed and under pressure, I don't communicate well at all. And in direct mailing, deadlines are relentless. [*Testing how much she can assume*] Have you ever been around a direct mail house?

Alice: No.

Marti: I should've explained that we have a drop coming down—that's how we refer to a mass mailing—and the mailing list printout was all messed up. When I said I couldn't talk with you, I meant only that we had alligators here, and I couldn't talk with you right then. I guess I didn't make myself clear. How do you feel about what I've just said?

Marti asks the last question to see if she is getting anywhere.

Alice: I guess I feel better about it. Sometimes I also assume that people hear what I mean, too. That *is* a mistake, isn't it?

Marti: True. Now, as for my old accounts, my boss asked only that I turn over some of the newer ones to the other salespeople, not the ones with a long-time relationship like ours.

Alice: Another wrong assumption. I'm sorry, again.

Marti: Well, I never told you that, and I should have. My replacement's hired, but she won't be on board for another week. I should've told you that, too. *My* apologies.

After a few seconds during which neither woman speaks, Marti takes a new tack.

Marti: Alice, being tied up with crises seems to be my main function as a supervisor. If this sort of thing happens again, what would you want me to say or do?

Alice: Listen, I've got alligators of my own. I'd understand if you said something like, "The alligators are biting. Let me get back as soon as I can." But, when it comes down to it, Marti, it's really not what you said. It's the way you said it that had me upset. Your tone of voice.

Marti: Short, abrupt. I understand. What you're asking for seems reasonable enough. I'll take more care with what I say and how I say it in the future.

Let's take a brief look at how Marti handled the conversation. No "er"s or "uh"s. Appropriate use of meaningful sounds. Ordinary, garden-variety words, with an immediate explanation of the one jargon phrase after testing Alice's familiarity with direct mailing.

What started out as a way to clarify what Marti meant by "I can't talk to you" turned into a process of cutting through several filtering factors: Marti's tone of voice and abruptness when pushed by pressures; Alice's feelings about that; and Alice's assumption about Marti's instructions. The end result was a feedback session in which Marti found out how her behavior affected Alice, how Alice felt about it, and what Alice needed from Marti to avoid that sort of incident in the future: Alice got the treatment Marti agreed was due her, and Marti set aside the bad feelings.

If Marti has to placate Alice too often, she may be buying into a game Alice plays. Only Marti can figure out if that's happening and put a stop to it. For more about game playing, see another book in this series, *How to Handle Difficult People.*

Marti's first step in getting control of her telephone environment was to get control of her own filters—to find out what she did to upset Alice. Unless she did that, she had no way of helping the other person get control over hers. She helped her telephone partner by listening effectively.

Chapter 3

Controlling Telephone Conversations by Listening

Before Marti attempted to clarify what had happened, she worked at her understanding of what her customer thought and felt by asking Alice to explain herself. She listened actively.

You gain more control over a phone conversation the more you listen in this special way. You let the

----

Active Listening

Participating in the other person's conversation by:
- Encouraging him/her to talk
- Asking questions for clarification
- Giving informational feedback
- Mirroring feelings and emotions

----

other person do most of the talking, but you participate in it and guide it. It's his or her own agenda, but it's discussed in the way you want him or her to do it. The outcome is a mutually satisfying collaboration for effective communication by seeing to it that both parties come away with what they want or need from the conversation.

When people start out with a disagreement or a conflict, as we saw in the dialogue between Marti and Alice, they use active listening for problem solving or managing the disagreement. Active listening is a management tool.

Effective listening doesn't mean sitting on one end of the line doing nothing while the party at the other end natters on endlessly; it means applying the 20 percent rule: You talk, but only 20 percent of the time.

In the previous dialogue, Marti asked the right questions for getting information or for confirming facts and opinions, gave informational feedback to reassure Alice she did understand, and mirrored Alice's feelings. She created the conditions that encouraged Alice to listen to her side. On the other hand, had Alice tried to dominate the conversation and persuade Marti to take her point of view or to do something different, Marti could have taken control of the conversation by turning Alice's questions or comments back on her.

Marti, in effect, had Alice resolve all the issues by getting her to explain what she experienced, why she felt the way she did about it, and what she would want Marti to do in the future. Alice was content with the answers *she* then got from Marti, but they addressed

- - - - - - - - - - - - - - - - - - -

Asking the Right Questions in the Right Way

- "When you said that, what did you mean?"
- "So, when you said that, you intended to
  get back as soon as possible. Is that right?"
- "How did you arrive at that?"

- - - - - - - - - - - - - - - - - - -

all of Alice's issues. The same techniques work well when you're on the phone to sell something or to convince someone you're right about something: Get the other person to tell you all the reasons why he or she should buy or agree with you. Match what you have to say to the responses you get.

Your questions, like those in the sidebar, probe for information; they clarify what the other person means or intends, and they cut through filters. Ask the right questions, the right way, and you'll get the answers you need without appearing to be the Grand Inquisitor. Your telephone partner convinces him- or herself that the buying decision or the agreement is the right thing to do.

When you ask people to explain what they mean, it helps the attempt to communicate if you provide informational feedback: paraphrasing what they said to reassure them that you do understand. By beginning your statement with a phrase similar to "If I understand what you're saying," or "It seems to me," you tell them you're taking responsibility for trying to understand what they're communicating.

It's only right that you give that assurance; at the same time, you get the opportunity to see if your interpretation is in fact correct. If you didn't catch on to what the person meant, he or she can correct you or elaborate on his or her point—do whatever it takes to complete the process and achieve closure.

If you think the other person is signalling feelings or emotions, your feedback should refer to them—mirror them. That way, you acknowledge what you hear and signify that you understand what you think the speaker is trying to get across to you. Especially if you pick up the feelings or emotions from the person's meaningful sounds, e.g., tone of voice, rather than from the words used, mirroring brings the feelings out in the open where you can deal with them. Saying "It seems you're upset" or "That seems to please you" lets the other person know you're tuning in both to what is being said and how that person feels about it.

Other people appreciate knowing that you understand how they feel about a situation or what they (or you) are saying. At the same time, you can find out if you're interpreting what you hear correctly.

Informational feedback and mirroring are checkpoints along the road to successfully communicating, and both informational feedback and mirroring help you create the conditions that encourage the other person to listen to you. That's what I mean by control. Control, you see, doesn't mean domination.

Control of an effective telephone conversation comes down to mutual respect. Showing the other person respect regardless of his or her beliefs, opinions, values, feelings, and emotions usually earns respect in return. (I did say "usually.") The person with whom you're talking usually returns the compliment of listening to you.

What if someone calls you with the intention of persuading you to take some point of view or do something but you're not sure you want to go along with it? You can gain control of the conversation by turning the statements back on that person.

Les, as graphic arts supervisor, talks regularly with clients about their logos or other packaging designs. On this occasion, the artist is talking with a man who wants a logo that does the impossible. In his words: "When a woman thinks of Lady Everett's Cosmetics, her heart beats harder, she breathes faster—a soaring eagle. A strong, swift, beautiful bird!"

"WRONG!" clangs in Les's mind, but not from his mouth.

Les: Everett, you want an image that excites a woman, that it?

Everett: Right.

Les:	That's important to you.
Everett:	Most important.
Les:	How will a flying bird do that?
Everett:	[*With pride and enthusiasm*] Well, it's not just a bird, it's an eagle.
Les:	And?
Everett:	It's America's symbol, and—well, you know, it's a strong, swift, beautiful bird.
Les:	Think about it, Everett. What kind of bird is an eagle?
Everett:	[*Confused*] What do you mean?
Les:	How does an eagle survive?
Everett:	[*Now not so sure of himself*] It lives on little animals—field mice, rabbits. Those things. [*Doubtful*] It's a bird of prey.
Les:	Right. What do you think, Everett? How many women want to see themselves as a bird of prey feeding on lesser animals?
Everett:	[*All enthusiasm for his idea gone*] I think I see what you're driving at.
Les:	You want to hear what I think?
Everett:	Sure, I think we've done in my idea.
Les:	My main point is, not many women want you to tell them that's what *you* think they are. Get twentieth century, Everett! That symbol'll kill you dead. Number one, women aren't birds of prey, and number two, tell 'em they are, and the last thing they'll do is buy your line of cosmetics.

Only when Everett was no longer tuned into his own point of view could Les give his opinion. For him to have tried while the customer was still feeling enthusiastic about his own idea would have escalated into an irresolvable debate. Les helps Everett to separate himself from a bad idea before offering his own opinion.

Les tactfully led Everett to talk about his own opinion. He asked the right questions or made the appropriate comments to bring his client to the point where he could offer an artist's opinion. Through his line of questioning, he acknowledged Everett's point of view before he launched into his.

When you take the time to help someone talk through his or her point of view, you're in a position to tailor your opinion to the other person's and not go off into irrelevant territory.

Les: Okay. Let's recap. You want a logo that will get a woman excited when she sees or hears the name Lady Everett's Cosmetics, right?
Everett: Right.
Les: Something beautiful.
Everett: Something beautiful. We can leave off the swift and strong.
Les: Okay. I think—

We really don't need to know what Les thinks. For all we know, it may be as sexist an idea as Everett's. What's important here is that by working someone through his or her own idea, you're in a better position to persuade that person to take a contrary viewpoint if you want to do so.

But to do that, you need to learn and practice some basic skills. Whether you play softball or want to improve your telephone listening skills, practice provides repetition and develops conscious habits. So every chance you get, use the listening tools described in the next chapter.

Chapter 4

Tools for Effective Listening on the Telephone

Winning on the telephone means using active listening to control and guide the conversation. It helps the other person meet his or her needs or requirements at the same time you meet yours. Not too long ago, the popular wisdom called this a win-win situation.

However, active listening does take some skill, and unless you practice certain specific techniques, you'll have trouble using it. These techniques include probes, encouragers, informational feedback, and behavioral feedback.

Probes

You saw how effectively both Marti and Les used questions to keep the other person talking and on track. Questions help you (1) get information (open-ended) or (2) confirm facts or opinions and end conversations (closed-ended).

An open-ended question can't be answered by a yes, no, or maybe. Usually beginning with a "w word"—*who, what, why, where, when*—or *how,* it demands some kind of informative response. Someone would sound silly answering yes, no, or maybe to "What happened yesterday?" The person might respond by saying "I don't know," but that's information, too.

Even "I don't know" keeps a conversation going. Other information-gathering questions could follow: "Where were you when it happened?" or "Who else was there?" And so on.

On the other hand, closed-ended questions usually end a conversation or some portion of it. They can be answered with yes, no, or maybe (as well as "I don't know"). Usually involving a "to be" or similar verb, they confirm facts or achieve closure. "Can you do this?" "Will you do this?" "Are you sure?" "Then we agree on this, right?" Not much can be said on the given subject after the other person answers these questions.

Gatekeepers

A variety of listening skills encourage people to talk (gatekeepers) by conveying your interest: open-ended

Probes
   • Open- and closed-ended questions

Gate-keepers:
   • Open-ended comments
   • Encouragers
   • Mirrors
   • Pregnant silence
   • Clarifiers
   • Feedback

-- -- -- -- -- -- -- -- -- -- -- -- -- -- --

comments, encouragers, mirrors, pregnant silences, clarifiers, and feedback.

Open-Ended Comments

Saying "Tell me more" specifically and directly tells the other person that you're interested in what he or she is saying. On the other hand, encouragers are more subtle.

Encouragers

"I see" or "uh huh" signal to the other person that you're listening and want more information. They draw the other person out, usually without him or her knowing what you've done. Mirrors, however, are as explicit as open-ended comments.

Mirrors

Mirrors reflect the other person's emotions or feelings. They are particularly effective when the other person has not made his or her emotions or feelings explicit. You have to pick up on them from tone of voice or word choice. For example, you may say, "I can hear how upset you are" or "You say you're pleased with the logo design." Such statements usually get the other person to expound on what he or she thinks or feels. That's also what a pregnant silence can accomplish.

Pregnant Silence

In physics we say that nature abhors a vacuum. In communication, silence creates a vacuum that people feel obligated to fill. A pregnant silence is a deliberate pause during which you wait for the other person to answer a question or respond to you in some way or to collect his or her thoughts. Unless the other person really doesn't care about you or about responding, he or she will answer quickly. Otherwise, he or she could wind up never answering.

Clarifiers

Clarifiers are something like open-ended comments insofar as they seek additional information, but this time, what you're looking for is more along the lines of an explanation: "Can you explain that further?" or "What does that mean to you?" When you ask for clarification, you usually get additional information as well.

Feedback

Finally, feedback can either encourage a person to talk more on the subject or shut down as if in answer to a closed-ended question. It all depends on how and when the feedback's given. Simply paraphrasing what the person said without significant interruption encourages. Like this:

Customer: I want a logo that clearly represents our services.

Les: A clear statement.

Customer:	Something sincere, classy. Simplicity's the name. It would help to highlight the name, I suppose.
Les:	Classical.
Customer:	You do understand, don't you, Les? I'm glad because—

On the other hand, the phrase "If I understand you, you're saying . . ." followed by a paraphrase of what the person said is the sort of feedback that evokes different responses.

When you give feedback and follow it with the question, "Is that right?" the person can answer either, "No, not exactly" or "That's it." In the first case, the speaker will usually correct your interpretation. In the second, he or she will probably accept your statement as a summary and assume that that part of the conversation has been completed—to have reached closure.

Summarizing works well when you've started off not really understanding what the other person said. After some discussion, you then say, "If I understand you, you mean . . ." and paraphrase what you think the other person meant. That way, you both can agree on the meaning of what was said. That, if you remember, is what communication is.

In addition to achieving closure around the meaning of something, summarizing helps bring a whole conversation or a portion of it to a close. It literally pulls all the ideas together and allows you to move forward into new territory.

When practicing these skills, be aware of several important do's that will help you achieve your telephone call objectives, and don't's that could interfere with your success on the telephone.

Do's and Don't's

No chapter on effective telephone listening skills is complete without a section with tips on how to maximize your effectiveness. Exhibit 2 lists the do's and don'ts of effective telephone communication. Read it before reading the remainder of the book.

Exhibit 2. Do's and don't's of effective telephone communication.

Do:	Don't:
• Show interest.	• Don't argue, even if you disagree.
• Make an effort to understand what the other person is trying to say.	• Don't interrupt unless you have a good reason.
• Make an effort to understand the other person's point of view (empathy) even if you don't agree with it.	• Don't pass judgment too quickly.
• Acknowledge the other person's viewpoint and let him or her know you disagree.	• Don't enter the conversation with preconceived ideas.
• Let him or her ask for your opinion.	• Don't give advice or behavioral feedback (i.e., tell the person how his or her behavior affects you) unless he or she is ready for it. Wait until you're asked.
• If a problem exists between you, try to identify it.	• Don't react to anger in kind; that only escalates bad feelings.
• Help the other person see the relationship between the cause and the problem.	
• Encourage the other person to solve his or her own problems.	
• Wait and listen when silence (pregnant silence) is the best answer.	

So much for listening on the phone. The space allocated to that topic indicates its importance—that what you say on the phone often depends upon what you hear. Still, much of your success on the phone will also depend on how well you express yourself.

Chapter 5

Keys to Getting Your Message Across

Effective self-expression on the telephone comes from being well prepared, the manner in which you express yourself, the way you articulate, and how you pace yourself.

Preparation

The Scouts have a phrase for it: Be prepared. When you make a call, even a social call, set an objective: What do you want to accomplish or get out of this call? Sometimes, especially in sales, it's wise to set a *primary* objective, e.g., get an appointment to see the decision-maker, and several secondary objectives, e.g., a time to call back or an opportunity to send literature.

To make sure you tell the other person everything you have to, list the main points in advance. Also treat any business call as if it's a meeting. Write down your agenda. A topic outline should serve you quite well.

Many new or inexperienced salespeople find cold-calling very difficult, partly because they don't know what they're going to say—if, indeed, they get past the secretary. If it's a first sales call, prepare an opening presentation. Just a few sentences should do it; in fact, you should not let your openers go on for more than thirty seconds before you get the other person talking.

Let's take a look at how Albert makes his cold calls. First of all, he knows in advance that the company on which he's calling manufactures packagable products.

He checks that out in his *Manufacturer's Guide*. He also knows that Mr. Jones is responsible for buying packaging materials; he checked that out by asking the receptionist the day before when he prepared his call list.

> Good morning, Mr. Jones. I'm Albert Barnes with Wilson Packaging. We produce all forms of plastic packaging, working with our clients to develop the art and execute the final product. To be sure we offer you the most cost-effective products and services you can find anywhere, I'll need to know how you package your products now. I have a few questions for you, Mr. Jones. Do you have a few minutes right now?

His opening presentation is designed to introduce himself, the name of his company, what his company can do for Mr. Jones (a benefit statement), and to get Mr. Jones talking. Once he gets Mr. Jones talking, he will use active listening to find out what this person's buying wants or needs are and what he's looking for from products, benefits, and services. His primary objective is to get an appointment to make a live presentation of how Wilson Packaging can meet the needs he uncovers during this discussion. Unless the caller is a telephone solicitor and must close the deal on the phone, that's what any successful, well-prepared salesperson does.

If Mr. Jones doesn't have "a few minutes" now, Albert will make an appointment to call back at a specific time—and keep it.

Successful salespeople also make very effective follow-up calls. Albert, for example, doesn't get on the phone without first writing out an objective and setting an agenda. He knows whom he wants to talk to, what he wants to talk about, and how he wants to talk about it. Any information he needs to give is in front of him. If he's trying to close a sale, he has trial closes ready. He's as ready as he can be to deal with possible questions, problems, and objections.

Stop and think about your own experience. You've received calls from hundreds of salespeople. You can separate the effective from the ineffective callers, can't you? Preparation does seem to be the great divider.

Obviously, it's different when someone calls you unexpectedly and wants your opinion or asks you to do something. When the shoe's on the other foot, when you're the recipient of a cold call, ask for time to think about what the caller has said (unless, of course, you're prepared to acquiesce). How many times has someone told you over the phone that this is a onetime, chance-in-a-lifetime opportunity? That the caller will never be able to offer this opportunity again? Nonsense! What makes the calling organization think you want anything that badly?

You can buy any product or service at any time, as long as the company or its competition stays in business. And most *reputable* firms will honor an opportunity offered over the telephone at any time.

If a business agenda's involved, in which you have to make a decision about something with which you're not familiar, ask for time to consider the proposition. A snap judgment made on the basis of a telephone conversation can lead you and your caller into a bad decision. Although I'm not suggesting you use this as an excuse for foot-dragging, it serves both your interest and the other person's to cool it until you've studied the issue.

Self-Expression

The more interesting your vocabulary, excluding jargon or technical language (unless they're appropriate), the more you'll hold your listener's attention. Most people appreciate hearing the mundane expressed in novel ways. (The mundane expressed in novel ways is one of the fascinations that television soaps hold over their audiences, according to some communication specialists.)

Now that doesn't mean using archaic, flowery, or affected language. Using action verbs rather than forms of the verb "to be" or similar weak verbs is a simple way of becoming more expressive. Look at these two sentences:

> The guide and I went into the room on the left.
> The guide led me into the room on the left.

Which sentence evokes the more interesting image?

Likewise, use the active rather than the passive voice. Here's the difference between the two:

> The lecture was delivered by the guide. [*Passive*]
> The guide delivered the lecture. [*Active*]

If you think of your subject as *doing* something, you should be able to communicate action and activity most of the time.

To be perfectly candid, most people ramble when they talk on the phone. They wouldn't use half the words to say something in a memo that they say into your ear. It doesn't seem fair, does it?

You can avoid that situation if you use short, simple, and complete declarative sentences to make your point. Think in discrete units, and when you prepare, check your units for conciseness. Wherever possible, avoid conjunctions: "and," "but," "either-or," "neither-nor." Look at these samples:

> The guide took us through the entire plant—the administrative offices as well as the manufacturing centers, the inventory and supply areas, the distribution and shipping areas—and then she showed us the R&D department, which, I've got to tell you, is the most sophisticated laboratory I've ever seen, and I think if we don't land this account, we're missing one whale of a bet, but I've the greatest confidence in Albert, and I think he'll do the job.

Now:

> The guide walked us through the entire plant. She showed us the administrative offices as well as the manufacturing centers. She also took us through the inventory and supply areas before we toured the distribution and shipping areas. The highlight of the day came when she led us into the R&D department. Now, I have to tell you,

I've never seen a more sophisticated laboratory. I think if we don't land this account, we're missing one whale of a bet. But I've got the greatest confidence in Albert. I think he'll do the job.

Exactly the same accounts, the one a breathy, run-on sentence, the other a well-paced, carefully stated narrative. Choosing the most effective presentation will make a difference in how your listener understands what you're saying.

The listener's understanding is, after all, your concern—it's your message. Closure's your responsibility. Therefore, not only should you express yourself carefully, you should check with the other person periodically to see if he or she does, in fact, understand you.

Take a look at another contrast:

Do you understand?

versus:

To make sure I've made myself clear, I need some feedback.

How will most people answer the first question, even if they really haven't understood at all? "Yep," "Sure," "Gotcha." Why? Because they're too embarrassed to say they haven't understood, or they really think they have. Either way, you've lost the whole ball game by asking the first question.

But the second question requires them to paraphrase what you've said to achieve closure. If they get it wrong, you can correct them. If they get it right, you're home free.

Articulation

Although it may not seem important, how you pronounce words advances your cause toward understanding and communication. Please articulate well, because if your listener can't understand your utterances, he or she can't understand their meaning.

Attack the beginning of your words cleanly and

clearly. Be careful not to swallow them—that is, don't drop your word endings or the last word of a sentence. Although I'm sure this is a needless piece of advice, don't chew gum or otherwise eat or drink anything while talking on the phone. You're chewing up your words at the same time, as well as showing a complete disregard for the other person.

Modulation

Nothing makes a conversation more uninteresting to a listener than a droning voice, especially if the discussion concerns technical data. When the listener loses interest, he or she also loses out on the meanings you intend. So, modulate. Change pitch periodically to avoid monotony.

You can speak dynamically by raising and lowering your *volume* appropriately. Some people shout on the phone. For some reason, they doubt that the wire can carry their voice, especially on long-distance calls. At the other extreme are people who have so much confidence in the power of electricity and electronics that they nearly whisper their messages. Neither group communicates very well.

Just speak in ordinary conversational tones, raising your voice to emphasize points, lowering it to create intimacy or secrecy. Of course, if you have a bad connection, throw this advice out the door.

Pace

Some people speak very rapidly; that seems to be a corollary of shouting, although I don't know why. Other people speak very slowly, which seems to be a corollary of monotone delivery.

Since you intend to modulate appropriately, vary your pace to fit the content or mood of what you're saying. When talking about something exciting, sound excited—but don't talk too fast for the other person to follow. When talking about something serious, sound serious—but don't slow things down to a sleep-inducing drone. You can accomplish either mood in part by prolonging vowels when the mood is serious and by quickening them when the mood is upbeat.

Telephone Vices and Fears

For some people, reaching out *properly* starts by reaching in. They have to gain control over their own abuse or disuse of the phone.

Telephone junkies spend much of their working hours making personal calls. On the other end of the line, *phonaphobes* can't handle the uncertainties the telephone produces. Whereas the first group can't control an addiction, the second group can't cope with a fear.

Telephonitis

Telephone junkies spend a large part of their day calling friends to talk about an upcoming dinner party or describe someone they met the night before; or else they phone the kids who are home from school because of Teachers Conference Day—not once, but four or five times between the personal calls coming in to them. If they have no reason to pick up the phone and call someone—while their work piles up or their customers languish—they invent one. All the while, they're being *paid.*

When such addicted employees finally get off the phone, the work is sloppily rushed—often during overtime (for which the employer also pays). Can you blame employers for thinking they're not getting value for the dollars they pay?

I'm not talking about the one call a day to a spouse, a loved one, or children, or the necessary calls to tradespeople who can't be reached at night; I'm talking about outright abuse. Increasing numbers of employers now think of this weakness of many otherwise skilled people as *stealing*—stealing *time,* which equates with money. Only by direct confrontation can a supervisor put a stop to such calls. Telling telephone junkies that they're stealing time from the company may be the sort of shock they need to begin trying to change their habits.

Still, the addict has to find his or her own way to kick the habit. One man uses this simple trick: Every time he feels the urge to call someone, he enters the person's name to a list labeled "Calls to Make Tonight." Usually he forgets to take the list home, and never makes the calls. Writing the note seems to satisfy the urge.

A nervous working mother's work nearly halted at 3:30 P.M. each day until her children agreed to call her when they came home from school. A five-minute conversation was enough to reassure her so that she could give her manager her undivided attention until 5:00 P.M. The woman's plan worked only because everyone agreed that after the one call, she would not accept another except in a dire emergency, and the *children scolded her* if she called them, except in a dire emergency, which they defined.

Phonaphobia

Tricks or strategies can't solve every telephone addict's problem, but correcting the situation of a person who uses the phone excessively may be easier than helping someone to cope with a fear of the telephone, or phonaphobia. Although it afflicts many professionals, it hits salespeople the hardest because they experience rejection more frequently than most people. Unless they truly believe that the prospects are rejecting not them but their products or services, their fear of rejection soon turns into a dread of picking up the phone.

To a phonaphobic salesperson, the receiver is an enormous monster waiting to suck the breath out of the lungs once it's placed near the mouth. The buttons fight back when they're punched. Anxiety dries the mouth, stains the underarms, and makes the world spin crazily. A promising career comes to an end.

Other people feel intimidated by people of "higher" status and have difficulty calling executive managers for an appointment. To them, the VIP's status may even rub off onto secretaries, and they have difficulty getting past a well-trained call-screener.

The stress of doing business with these people also contributes to phonaphobia. Soon, phonaphobics find making a call more difficult than communicating in other ways. They write a letter when a call is the obvious and better way of handling a situation.

Overcoming phonaphobia takes some effort. The more severe it is, the less likely the person will succeed. Still, except in the most hopeless of cases, these pointers can help:

1. Recognize that rejection or resistance is a part of the business game. For a salesperson, selling doesn't begin until the customer says no.
2. Recognize also that people at the other end of the line are just ordinary human beings. No matter what their title or position, they're just like you—forced to put their socks on one foot at a time. Especially if they have to make decisions about the matter for which you are calling, they may be even more scared than you are. Act and talk the way you'd like them to act and talk, and you'll probably make out just fine.
3. To make out at all, give yourself a better reason for picking up the handset than for not picking it up. Set a goal for yourself: making an appointment, getting a decision. Then set two or three backup objectives you're willing to accept: a time to call back, a promise to reach a decision by tomorrow. Come away with *something* you need or want every time you make a call, and the next call won't seem so tough to make.

People can control their misuse or fear of the telephone and they can gain control over how they use it, but they can't expect other people always to respect their right to control it. There are some callers on whom nothing seems to make an impression, and those are the people discussed in the next chapter.

Chapter 6

How to Handle Problem Callers

What could be more trying on a busy day than getting an unwanted call from a phone sales or solicitation person? Especially from one who says:

> Hello, Mr. Hobart. My company, XYZ Art Seminars, has a full series of workshops on how to communicate effectively through graphics. We have programs on—

Or how about the Angry Caller?

> Marti, Les did it to me again! Everytime I call and he answers the phone, I can just bet he won't leave a message. Now, I called yesterday, and you haven't called back, so obviously he didn't leave the message. I just don't know what to—

Of course, the opposite of that is the Playful Caller:

> Albert? This is Frank from Penn Pens. How's it going, good buddy? Listen, before I get into why I called, I just gotta tell you the joke I heard the other day—from one of your competitors, no less. It seems there were this priest, this rabbi, and this minister on an airplane. Now stop me if you've heard it.
>
> I've heard it, Frank, but I wouldn't repeat it.

You've listened to the Ear Bender for hours, no doubt:

> Marti? Joyce Keiper, from Schillers. Let me tell you what happened here just yesterday. Jane—

You know, Mr. Allen's secretary? She had a big fight with her husband right in the office, and it stirred up quite a fuss. Well, I told her—You know she talks to me about everything, like I'm her mother. Well, older sister, anyway.

Then, there's the Strong, Silent Caller:

Hello, Mr. Friendly. I know you're there. I can hear you breathing.

Love 'em all, don't you?

You can control these problem callers, too. It doesn't take much, just the late Averell Harriman's diplomatic tact and Mother Teresa's saintly patience.

Unwanted Phone Sales or Solicitations

This category does *not* include calls you need to receive in order to supply your office, provide inventory for your plant, and so forth. Unwanted phone sales or solicitations include only those calls in which you're not interested. You don't want or need the offer, period.

How do you respond to this type of caller? Say you don't need what he or she has to offer and hang up.

You don't take a blasé or glib attitude. You turn the caller down tactfully. For example:

Listen, Ms. Smythe. I appreciate your call, and to save you precious time, let me tell you, we don't have a budget for your services at this time. Thank you for calling.

It's a fair, honest, and tactful response. It also ends the conversation in less than a minute.

The Angry Caller

If you have a reason for listening to an angry caller, you really don't have much choice. If he or she is a customer or the boss, hang in calmly and empathetically.

Unless you've done something to anger the person,

he or she is not angry with you but, rather, with a situation or a problem. The caller wouldn't have tapped you unless he or she felt confident of getting results—or at least an understanding ear. So until the person has blown off steam, listen. Let the caller ventilate the feelings until he or she has, as the psychologists say, "drained the pain."

Let the person know you understand what he or she's saying. Acknowledge the feelings by mirroring: "I can hear how angry you are." But *never* agree: "You're right to feel angry." Once you agree, you'll have a devil of a time getting the caller past the anger.

It's the same as agreeing with a customer's objection to your product or services. Agree and the objection is validated and set in concrete.

As hard as it may seem, be pleasant. Even if the person is angry with something you've done or said, the caller has a right to his or her feelings, even if the perceived injury is a mirage. You'll get your day in court, but only if you maintain your cool under fire.

You get nowhere by answering in kind; you can only escalate the bad feelings. But you don't have to tolerate crude or obscene anger.

> Mr. Johnson. I'm willing to deal with your complaint, but I'm not willing to take this kind of verbal abuse. If you don't stop, I will terminate the call.

And, if the caller doesn't cease and desist, hang up. It's your phone.

Only when the pain has been drained, and only at that point, will you gain control of the conversation. While the other person is ventilating, there's no way he or she can tune in to what you're saying. Judge the timing and get control by probing. Let's see how Marti handles Alice's newest challenge:

Alice: —so obviously he didn't leave the message I gave. I just don't know what to—

Marti: Alice, let me break in a second. You do seem pretty steamed.

Alice:	Yes, I am. And you'd be, too, if Les kept doing this to you.
Marti:	Now, you want me to do something about it, right?
Alice:	Of course I do.
Marti:	Then, let's see if Les did anything wrong, okay?
Alice:	Well, I left a message, and you haven't called back.
Marti:	When did you call, Alice?
Alice:	Yesterday, at 4:15 or so.
Marti:	And Les answered the phone?
Alice:	Yes.
Marti:	Okay. Here's the message, Alice. He wrote, "Call Alice tomorrow if not today." I just haven't gotten to it, yet.
Alice:	Oh, well, uh—

The most important thing that Marti does is to cut Alice off in an appropriate way, at an appropriate time (Alice's intensity wavered with "I just don't know what to—"), and show her willingness and ability to help solve the problem. Once you sincerely demonstrate that bit of personal concern, the other person's anger is gone forever.

The Playful Caller

In the example quoted at the beginning of this chapter, Albert takes a direct and blunt approach to a customer who is repeating a joke in bad taste. In such cases, one of two things will happen, depending on the relationship you've established with that person. Either the caller will hang up and never call back, or the person will realize that the joke is in bad taste and drop it. You have to be the judge of your relationship and its value.

If you *must* deal with this person no matter what, remain sober but not unfriendly or cold. Laugh with him or her if it's appropriate, but gain control as soon as you can by probing for the real reason for the call and for information.

It's interesting to note that many times a caller's

humor comes from nervousness over a problem or a complaint. The person feels intimidated by the circumstances and tries to joke through them. If, when you probe, you find that a problem exists, show your willingness and ability to help solve the problem. The caller will relax and the joking will stop.

The Ear Bender

Did you ever call for directions to a meeting and get someone's full life story? Some people take every opportunity to gab they can get. They rationalize it by saying they want to get to know people better, but they never really give you the opportunity to say anything. How can *they get to know you* that way?

If you have to deal with this person, patiently wait for the first opening to take control, first by acknowledging what he or she has said, and then by using mostly closed-ended questions and comments.

Above all, avoid gatekeepers of any kind, e.g., pregnant silences, open-ended questions, or encouragers. Give that much attention to irrelevant gab, and the person will never shut up.

Let's take a look at how Marti handled her second caller.

Joyce: —well, older sister, anyway.

Marti: That's really nice, Joyce. I suppose a lot of the younger women there look up to you and seek your advice.

Joyce: Well, yes. I suppose they do.

Marti: It's really fortunate for them that they have you there to talk with. Now, how can I help you?

Marti jumps in the first moment Joyce pauses for a short breath. Otherwise, she would have been on the phone forever. Once more, if a problem surfaces, she'll show her willingness and ability to help solve the problem. Once the Ear Bender has his or her attention tuned in to the reason for his call, the chatter is sure to end.

The Strong, Silent Caller

What's deadlier than dead silence? I've talked about that in Chapter 4. We know that nature abhors a vacuum. Pregnant silence? That's one thing. Dead air? That's another matter altogether.

You may have to deal with a person who calls, probably because he or she has a problem or is upset about something but doesn't know how to communicate about it. Be patient. At this moment, Mr. Friendly finds even the breathing you hear difficult.

Use mostly open-ended questions and comments. Don't put the caller through the third degree of a battery of closed-ended questions. Make the strong, silent caller answer, even if your pregnant silences seem to take forever. Otherwise, you may wind up in a game of twenty questions that could extend to forty or more.

After this caller says something, summarize it. Summarize frequently. Each time he or she hears that he or she has made a point, it provides positive reinforcement and loosens up the person's tongue. And, again, the more you show your willingness and ability to help solve the problem, the more the person will talk about it.

Conclusion

A telephone call: an attempt to produce complete communication in an incomplete environment. That's no easy task. It requires control over factors that seem almost out of your control.

The way you encode or decode messages, the way you manipulate your own communication filters and the way you help the other person manipulate his or hers all enter into the process at one time or another. Begin by knowing yourself. And get the help of a friendly feedback partner.

Then, listen actively. Maintain control of the conversation by asking the right questions, using gatekeepers effectively to encourage the other person to talk, and summarizing what you think the other person has said. Ask the other person for feedback, also. That's how you achieve closure.

When you speak, be prepared. Be articulate, and articulate well. A good vocabulary well enunciated helps communicate competence and self-confidence. Modulate your voice and pace your delivery so that it is appealing to the listener; he or she will listen.

If you have problems with a caller who won't listen, maintain control of your own feelings and emotions (your filters). Unwanted calls? Get rid of them quickly but politely. Usually, you need only the proper questioning to get an angry, playful, or strong, silent caller to display appropriate behavior.

A simple rule of thumb? Winning on the telephone begins by taking control of how you use the phone and ends with sharing a mutually beneficial objective with your telephone partner.

INDEX

55

ABOUT THE AUTHOR

Donald H. Weiss, Ph.D., of Millers' Mutual Insurance in Alton, Illinois, has been engaged in education and training for over twenty-six years and has written numerous articles, books, audiocassette/workbook programs, and video training films on effective sales and supervisory or management skills. He speaks regularly on stress management and other personal development subjects, and has produced a variety of related printed or recorded materials.

During his career, Dr. Weiss has been the manager of special projects for a training and development firm, the manager of management training for an insurance company, the director of training for an employment agency group, a training consultant, and a writer-producer-director of video training tapes. He also has taught at several universities and colleges in Texas, including the University of Texas at Arlington and Texas Christian University, in Fort Worth.

Currently, Dr. Weiss is corporate training director for Millers' Mutual Insurance.